DAILY PRAYERS

A Classic Collection

F. B. MEYER

Harold Shaw Publishers
Wheaton, Illinois

Copyright © 1995 by Harold Shaw Publishers

Originally published in 1913 as *My Daily Prayers* by Fleming H. Revell Company. Some wording in this edition has been updated.

ISBN 0-87788-169-3
Cover photo ©1995 by Harold Shaw Publishers
Cover and inside design ©1995 by David LaPlaca

Library of Congress Cataloging-in-Publication Data

Meyer, F.B. (Frederick Brotherton), 1847-1929
    [My daily prayer]
    Daily prayers : a classic collection / F.B. Meyer.
        p.   cm.
     Originally published: My daily prayer. London : National Council
of the Evangelical Free Churches, 1913.
     ISBN 0-87788-169-3
     1. Prayers. 2. Devotional calendars.   I. Title.
    BV260. M4 1995
     242' .2–dc20   95-7949
                                                    CIP

02   01   00   99   98   97   96   95

10 9 8 7 6 5 4 3 2 1

JANUARY

1. Be with me, Lord, as I step out on the untrodden way of this new year. I know not what it may bring of joy or sorrow, of temptation or service; but I humbly commit myself and my way to you. Make the best that you can of me for your glory.

2. I bless you, O Son of God, that there is no need for me to go up to heaven to bring you down or into your grave to bring you up. You are here, in this hour and at this place. I confess you as Lord and believe in my heart that you are risen from the dead.

3. You have said, O Lord Jesus, that anyone who believes in you has ever-lasting life. I do now believe. With my whole heart I look to you as Savior, Friend, and King; and in this glad hour I receive from your hand not only life, but life more abundantly.

4. Deliver me, O my Lord from self-confidence, self-centeredness, and self-consciousness. You be my confidence, and the center of my activities; and may I always be more conscious of your presence than of the presence or absence of others.

5. Fix my heart, O Lord, on you, that amid the changes and chances of this mortal life I may be kept steadfast and immovable, ever abounding in your work.

6. Lord Jesus, who knows the weakness of my mortal nature, take away from me the fear of death; and when I come to the last, open for me the beautiful gate of life, that I may pass through it into the eternal Temple of God.

7. Lord, it is not in us to direct our ways. I pray that I may never lean to my own understanding; but, trusting in you with all my heart, may I be led in the way everlasting.

8. Fill me with your joy, O Lord, that I may have the means by which to give to my home and friends and to the great, sad world around me. Keep me from hiding my light under the bushel of my own anxieties.

9. Help me, dear Lord, to walk in the footsteps of your holy life, denying myself and becoming poor, that those around me may be made rich. Teach me how to gain by giving, and to find by losing, according to your Word.

10. My heart, O my God, is broken and contrite for all the sin and failure of my life. I can only bring it to you as my best sacrifice; and I thank you for your promise not to despise it.

11. Make me, O blessed Master, strong in heart, full of courage, fearless of danger, holding pain and peril cheap when they lie in the path of duty. May I be strengthened with all might by your Spirit in my inner being.

12. Almighty God, speed your gospel around the world, that all nations may soon have heard its glorious message; and may your strayed flock come back to the one fold—your heart, and to the one Shepherd— your only-begotten Son.

13. By day and by night, in life and in death, may I ever be true to you, O Lover of my soul, my ceaseless Friend, my unchangeable Savior. Into your hands I commit my soul.

14. I turn to you, O merciful God! To whom else could I go? My sins are many, but your mercy is great; my sins are swift, but your anger is slow; my tears are bitter, but your tenderness is sweet and sure. Let your gentleness make me great.

15. O God my Father, to you nothing is small and nothing great; the ages are as sands on the shore and nations as drops in the bucket. Help me to look not at this affliction, which is but for a moment, but to the far exceeding and eternal weight of glory.

16. Grant me, O Lord, I pray, a keen sensitiveness to all that is beautiful in nature and lovely in my fellow human beings, that I may see your beauty everywhere and be changed into your image.

17. Make me, O divine Friend, strong and pure in my friendship, that I may never break down barriers which I ought to maintain or withhold that which I ought to give for the help and comfort of others.

18. Give me grace, O you who were tempted in all points as we are and yet did not sin, to be watchful against the earliest and most insidious approaches of temptation, that I may at once hide myself under the shadow of your wings.

19. Open to me, O Spirit of Truth, the treasures of your holy Word, that my soul may be continually enriched, and that I may abound in every good word and work.

20. O gracious Giver of all things, enable me ever to remember that whatever you have given is a sacred trust to be held and used for others. May I have the humble consciousness that I have glorified you on the earth and finished the work which you gave me to do.

21. Teach me to love your beautiful world as you loved it, to whom the mountains, flowers, and birds ministered. Speak to me through all the voices of nature, and grant me a quick sensitiveness to your presence beneath its pure and transparent veil.

22. Withhold me, O holy Savior, from all filthiness of the spirit, as well as of the flesh, that I may gain perfect holiness in the fear of the Lord.

23. Most blessed Comforter, weary not of me, who am often weary of myself. My only hope is in your love, which loves to the uttermost. Prepare yourself yet once again, and wash my soiled life. You will not quench the smoking wick nor break the bruised reed.

24. May I never profess more than I actually experience; but may the hidden things of my heart be richer and fuller and deeper than I express to any but to you, O searcher of hearts.

25. Come to me, Lord, in my brokenness. My fair ideals are like trampled flowers, and my attempts after perfection have failed; but do for me what I cannot do for myself. Perfect that which concerns me, because your mercy endures forever.

7

26. Deliver me, O Lord, from every false way, that I may cling to you with a perfect heart, and so by your mercy may know you, as also I am known by you, through Jesus Christ.

27. Be my ruler and guide, gracious Father, that I may pass through temporal things in such a way as not to lose the things eternal.

28. Enrich me, O Lord, by the many gifts of your Holy Spirit, that I, patiently enduring through the darkness of this world, and being filled by your heavenly grace, may become a burning and shining light until the day dawns and the shadows flee away.

29. Help me to deny myself, and be crucified to the world, that I may follow the Lamb wherever he goes, lifting up my head with holy joy, because the day of my redemption draws near.

30. By your holy inspiration, O Lord, enlighten my understanding, direct my heart and mind, keep my lips, and reveal yourself to me in the riches of your grace and glory.

31. Teach me, O Lord, to discern your will and to faithfully and diligently perform it, that my life may be to your glory.

FEBRUARY

1. Grant, O Lord, to me and all your saints, the fullness of joy from your presence and the treasures of goodness which are at your right hand.

2. Heavenly Father, I pray that Jesus Christ may become dearer to me. May I love him as a personal friend and hide myself in the hourly awareness of his presence. May I have no taste or desire for things which he would disapprove. Let his love constrain me not to live for myself, but for him.

3. Fulfill in me, I pray, all the good pleasures of your goodness, and the work of faith with power.

4. May I be enabled to drink of your cup and be baptized with your baptism, that I may be near you when you come in your kingdom.

5. Heavenly Vine! Pour your vital sap through all the arteries of my soul, that I may bear much fruit for your glory.

6. Most holy God, in whose sight even the heavens are not clean, spare me not until my heart is cleansed, purified, and sanctified, that I may not seem better to others than I am toward you.

7. Help me so to live that those especially associated with me, and directing or serving me day by day, may long to have the love and joy which they see in me.

8. My all is now surrendered to you, my Lord; make of me as much as possible for your glory.

9. I long to arrange my will on your side, O my God; keep it there, that I may hate what you hate, forsake what you would have me forsake, and do what you call me to accomplish.

10. Give me, most gracious Lord, singleness of heart, that in every word, thought, and deed I may put you first and in all humility and earnestness seek to serve you, and you only.

11. Impart to me, heavenly Father, I pray, a self-forgetful spirit, that I may be more anxious to give than to receive, more eager to understand than to be understood, more thoughtful of others, more forgetful of myself.

12. Send me, O Lord, I humbly ask, good success this day. Teach me when to speak and when to be silent; when to act and when to refrain from action; and in all the details of daily life, to do your will on earth as it is done in heaven.

13. If today I should get lost amid the perplexities of life and the rush of many duties, search me out, gracious Lord, and bring me back into the quiet of your presence.

14. Give me grace, O my Father, to persevere in the work to which you have called me, neither leaving it half-done nor giving up when the first enthusiasm has faded and other interests attract.

15. Calm me, O God, when my spirit is feverish and hot. Place your cool hand upon my head; breathe the spirit of your calm through my heart. May I know that around my restlessness, you are rest.

16. Make me, O holy Father, so quick to respond to the pruning of the silver knife of your internal dealings with my soul that I may be spared from bleeding under the iron knife of external pain.

17. O heavenly Father, unveil to me, I humbly ask, the sweet mystery and beauty of your name —Abba Father.

18. May I so yield to you, as you wrestle with and overcome my proud nature, that I may be enabled to prevail with God and others.

19. You who were meek and lowly in heart, may I be genuinely humble with the humility which does not realize that it is humble.

20. Teach me to lose the personal in the universal and to be as triumphant in the successes of others, in which I have no share, as in my own.

21. Fill me, I entreat you, with such an absorbing passion for your kingdom and glory that I may be eager for you to be glorified, though I die unrecognized and unknown.

22. Help me to believe that all things are from you and that you have a plan for my life, in which each passing incident has a part.

23. May I give, not things only, but myself to others, with full measure, heaped up and running over. May I despair of no one, and look for nothing in return.

24. I bring to you, O Lord, my desires, and pray that you will cleanse them by the searching fires of your pure Spirit, that I may desire only those things which you have chosen and prepared for me.

25. Eternal God, work in me not only to will but to do your good pleasure; and may I work out what you work in me.

26. Heavenly Father! Take into your loving care my home, my loved ones far and near, and all members of your great scattered family. Let me not be anxious about tomorrow's provision or path, but trust you to provide and lead. Open your hand and satisfy the desire of every living thing.

27. I pray, O my Father, that you would help me to have a simpler and more confiding faith. May I trust more than I know and believe more than I see; and when my heart is overwhelmed within me, lead me to the Rock that higher than I.

28. Help me, Father, to believe that tomorrow is in your hands, that you will be with me, and that as my days, so shall my strength be.

29. Send me, gracious Lord, the Comforter. May he fill my nature as the rain fills the pools; and may the parched ground of my heart become as a garden. Instead of the thorn may there come up the fir tree, and instead of the briar, the myrtle.

MARCH

1. Blessed Lord! As far as it lies in my power, may I live peaceably with all people. Teach me to commit my cause to you, who judges righteously, not anxious to defend or avenge myself, but always more anxious to set an example of enduring patience than to manifest the strength of our cause.

2. Lord God Almighty, look on those to whom the world is dark; send a ray of light to gladden the lonely and sad-hearted, the forsaken and forgotten, the sinful and miserable; and teach me how to comfort them with the comfort you have given me.

3. O Savior, who goes after those who are lost until you find them, teach me to minister to the needs of others. May I compassionately regard those who do not know you and whose lives are one long outrage against your forbearing love. Give me something of your Shepherd compassion and longsuffering.

4. My Father God, let the motto of my life henceforth be "Glory to God in the highest," for only so can there be peace in my heart and goodwill towards others. May my heart be kept in unison with the angels' song.

5. Set a guard, O Lord, at the door of my lips, that I may speak nothing inconsistent with perfect truth and love.

6. Gracious God, let me behold the rainbow of hope on the dark stormclouds that brood over my life; and may I rest confidently on that covenant, ordered and sure, which was sealed by the precious blood of Christ.

7. O King of glory and Lord of hosts, who has ascended in triumph to the right hand of the Father, do not leave me comfortless, but send me the promise of the Father, even the Spirit of Truth.

8. As Jesus my Lord ascended into the heavens, so grant me, merciful Father, that I also, in heart and mind, may ascend and dwell with him continually.

9. Cause me, O God, I humbly pray, to be inflamed with heavenly desires. May your love be so strong in my heart that I will evermore seek the things which are above, where Christ sits at your right hand.

10. Help me, O Lord, to add to my faith, strength; and to strength, knowledge; and to knowledge, self-control; and to self-control, endurance; and to endurance, godliness; and to godliness, brotherly kindness; and to brotherly kindness, love. May these be in me and abound.

11. Teach me not only to bear, but to love your Cross. And as I take and carry it, may I find that it is carrying me.

12. Grant me concentration of purpose and singleness of heart, that I may do, not many things, but much. Cause my heart to fear and serve you.

13. Heavenly Father, have mercy on those who do not know you; take from them all ignorance, hardness of heart, and contempt of your Word. So bring them home, blessed Lord, to your flock, that they may be saved and become one flock under the Great Shepherd and Bishop of souls.

14. Almighty God, I ask you to raise me from the death of sin to the life of righteousness by that same power that brought the Lord Jesus from the dead, that I may walk in newness of life and be planted in the likeness of his resurrection.

15. Heavenly Father, I know that all things are working together for my good; but help me to wait patiently and work diligently, though the waiting be long and the toil hard.

16. O Lord, there is nothing in me that can attract or hold your love. I have failed often, and cost you much. Forgive my bitter past, and make me beautiful in the beauty which you will place upon me.

17. Heavenly Father, I thank you for the trials and pains that are ever working for my good and that are making me a partaker of your holiness. May I receive the abundance of your grace and reign in life here and hereafter.

18. Most gracious God, make me alive me by your Holy Spirit, I pray, that I may run in the way you have marked out for me, with earnest desire. Give me preparedness and alertness, and may I ever keep looking to Jesus.

19. Holy Father, I thank you for your forgiving, compassionate love. I gratefully realize that our sin cannot alter your love, though it may dim our enjoyment of it. But I ask you to set me free from the love and power of sin, that it may not intercept the light of your countenance.

20. O Savior, may I be permitted not only to touch the hem of your garment, but also to lean back on your heart. May I be one whom you love.

21. Heavenly Father, make me like Jesus, who, though he was rich, for our sakes became poor, that many through his poverty might be made rich. Help me to deny myself, so as to give joy and comfort to those less favored than I am; and may I learn how much more blessed it is to give than to receive.

22. Amid the temptations of the Evil One, and the provocation of the ungodly, help me to stay steadfast and immovable, so as to be counted worthy to stand before the Son of Man.

23. May the Holy Spirit bring all things to my remembrance, when in the heat of passion or the stress of life I am tempted to forget.

24. When temptation is near, may I meet it as a soldier who is conscious that the captain is fighting at his side.

25. Withdraw my soul, I pray, from the absorbing delight of this world, with its petty aims and ideals, and open my eyes to the high joys of my inheritance in Christ.

26. Holy Spirit, teach me to put away anger, wrath, malice, and evil communications, loveless words and loveless acts, and may I put on a heart of compassion, kindness, humility, meekness, longsuffering. May I forbear with and forgive others as you bear with and forgive me.

27. Hasten the coming of your kingdom, O Lord, the fulfillment of your promise, and the consummation of your purpose, that the pain of this world may soon usher in the rest of your eternal Sabbath.

28. Lord Jesus, teach me to see the good even in bad things; to discern the silver edge of lowering clouds; and to believe in your love, which is conducting me safely and by a right way to my home.

29. Heavenly Father! You kill and make alive; you bring down to the grave and bring up; you raise up the poor from the dust and lift the needy from despair, to make them sit in heavenly places and inherit the throne of God. Glory to you, O Most High!

30. Lord Jesus, as you loved Jerusalem, teach me to love my homeland. I pray for our leaders and the rulers of other lands; for statesmen, judges, magistrates, and all in authority; that we may be quietly and godly governed; and that peace and happiness, truth and justice, religion and piety may be established among us for all generations.

31. I would not hide or cloak my sins before your face, Almighty God, my heavenly Father; but confess them with a humble, penitent heart; so that I may receive forgiveness through your infinite goodness and mercy.

APRIL

1. Most blessed Lord! Have mercy upon those who have rejected the invitation of your gospel, and to whom it has become an aroma of death. Help those who have missed their religious privileges because of sickness or bereavement, or some other cause known to you.

2. Most gracious God, I thank you for the gift of the Holy Spirit, the Comforter, pure as dew, cleansing as fire, tender and refreshing as the breath of spring. O blessed Trinity, ever engaged in giving your choice things to us, your unworthy children, accept my gratitude.

3. May my heart be so child-like and pure that I may see the beauty of the world around me as it appears to the eyes of angels and as it appeared to you, my Lord, when you noticed the lilies and the birds.

4. May I not only find forgiveness in your cross, my blessed Lord, but may it produce in me rivers of living water, as the rod of Moses drew them from the rock.

5. Heavenly Father! Help me to remember that what you have given, you will require; and enable me so to live that I may multiply the talents with which you have entrusted me, by using them for your glory and for the comfort and help of others.

6. My Savior, may I unload your ships as they come, richly freighted, for my need. May I rejoice in all the good you send and be receptive of all things that pertain to life and godliness, that my character may abound in gold, silver, and precious stones.

7. Oh, to be wholly yours! I would have no thought closed from your Spirit; no act other than you would approve; no word inconsistent with your perfect love; no purpose in which you cannot have a part.

8. May I not be satisfied with talking or musing on your love. Grant me the grace to manifest it, not only in great crises, but amid petty annoyances and daily worries.

9. Help me to meditate more intently on your humility and patience, O my Savior, so that almost unconsciously these traits may reappear in my own character.

10. Holy Father! In you everything is found that can make your children glad, and I praise you with my whole being. You have kept me while I slept, so that I might awaken in safety, and to you I would consecrate my renewed strength. Let my heart, this morning, rejoice.

11. I pray to you, O Lord, to give me a ready sympathy with others, that I may look at things from their standpoint and see myself as they see me.

12. Show me today, O Lord, that one to whom I am to give a cup of cold water in your name.

13. Let me not dwell on the past, my Father, as though it held the best. May I dare to believe that the best is yet to be, and that though you are filling my life with the rain of tears, every one of them will one day yield the wine of joy.

14. Lord Jesus, I thank you that a new day affords another opportunity for consecration and devotion. You have turned a fresh page in my life's story. It comes from you without blemish or soil; help me to keep it so. Forgive the past blotted with my failures and sins, and help me to walk in the light.

15. Make me, O Lord, to know the hope of your calling, the riches of the glory of your inheritance in the saints, and the exceeding greatness of your power toward those who believe. Above all, grant me the spirit of wisdom and revelation in the knowledge of yourself.

16. Help me, O Lord, to appreciate the sensitiveness of your love. May I not disappoint you by using exaggerated outward expressions of that personal relationship which is slowly growing between us.

17. Lord, I cannot hope to sit on your right or your left hand in your kingdom, nor to lean on your bosom, but at least permit me to sit at your feet and hear your word.

18. Father, I know that you suffer in our suffering, and that your sympathy is quick and tender and deep. Thank you that our blessed Lord has wept human tears, and borne the weight of human sorrow. May I comfort others with the comfort I have received from you.

19. Make yourself so real to me that my first thought in everything will be to do your will and to avoid whatever might give you sorrow.

20. Let me not be satisfied with refraining from sin; but as I abide in you, may I bear the fruits of the Spirit, which are love, joy, and peace.

21. May I be quick to discern in each person I meet how I can help you in freeing that soul still more from sin and lifting it to a life of righteousness.

22. Heavenly Father! Forgive my many sins, ignorances, and failures and cleanse me from all sin for the sake of Jesus Christ our Lord. Accept me graciously, and love me freely. May I hate sin as you do, and may your grace sink deeper into my heart, purifying the springs of thought and action.

23. Teach me, my Savior, to understand the meaning of your Cross, that through death with you there to every sin, I may enter with you into the fullness of life.

24. Most gracious God! Wherever at this hour there is sickness in home or hospital; wherever souls are passing from time to eternity; wherever there is anguish, peril, and alarm, may your gentle Holy Spirit be there, instilling peace and help. I ask it in the name of Jesus Christ.

25. Most blessed Lord! Hear me for those I love, especially for those who are passing through the valley of the shadow and to whom the day brings no alleviation of pain or sorrow. Put gladness into their hearts; may light arise in their darkness; and let the days of their mourning be ended.

26. O send out your light and your truth, and let them lead me and bring me at last to my Father's house in peace.

27. Make me a bright Christian, I entreat you, not morbid and austere and silent, not foolish and frivolous, but radiant, glad, and happy.

28. Holy Father! Give me grace to lay aside the works of darkness and to put on the armor of light. May all self-indulgence, all that is earthly, selfish, and unholy, be put away; and may I not fail you in the day of battle!

29. Give me, my Father, a loving and thankful heart. May your mercies, like cords, bind me to the horns of your altar. Let nothing be held back from you; but may my entire nature be surrendered to your indwelling and service, like a palace in which every room is freely open to its Lord.

30. O Heavenly Father, help me consider the interests of others and act nobly and generously towards them, because we are all your children, and your infinite resources are at our command. Make me a blessing to those I come in contact with, that I may leave upon their lives some trace of that light that I have caught from the face of Christ.

MAY

1. I pray to you, Lord, to deliver me from the fear of death. When my eyes open in the dawn of heaven, may I see you standing to welcome me; and may I receive your "Well done."

2. Keep me through this day from all that would grieve your Holy Spirit. Help me to look, not on the dark cloud, but on your rainbow; not on the stormy waters, but on the face of Jesus; not on what you have taken or withheld, but on what you have left; not on my own fickle and changing heart, but on your love, which is steadfast as the great mountains.

3. For all your bounties known to me, Heavenly Father, and for all the gifts unknown, accept my hearty thanks. May I not complain in your providence or dread the unknown future. Whatever befalls me, help me to believe in your unfailing care and to know that in the valley of the shadow you are by my side.

4. Help me never to break your confidence, my God, or to complain to others that your discipline is too severe.

5. May I anoint my head and wash my face that I may not appear to others to suffer, but only to you, who sees in secret and who will reward me openly.

6. Keep me from running here and there for human sympathy. May I be satisfied with you. Whom have I in heaven but you? And earth has nothing I desire besides you.

7. I ask you, Lord, to give me your Holy Spirit in greater measure, that his saving presence may cleanse my conscience and his holy inspiration enlighten my heart.

8. Take from my heart, Heavenly Father, all hatred and malice, all envy and jealousy, and everything which would cause a breach between me and others; that nothing may prevent the inflowing of your love to my heart and its outflowing towards others.

9. Since it is your will, my God, that I should suffer, give me patience, gentleness, and forgetfulness of myself; and thus help me to minister joy and blessing to others.

10. Give me grace, Heavenly Father, to administer well for the benefit of others those gifts which you have entrusted to me, that I may be a good steward of your many mercies and not be ashamed before you at your coming.

11. Let me not hesitate to come to you, even when a shameful fall is fresh. May I dare to believe in your immediate forgiveness and in my restoration to the old standard in your dear presence.

12. Ah, Lord, my love is like some feebly-glimmering spark; I desire it to be like a hot flame. Kindle it by your breath, until your love constrains me!

13. I pray to you, gracious Lord, that I may not miss any of those lessons which you desire to teach me by your Spirit, your Word, and your providence.

14. Help me, O Lord, to believe that what seems to be my losses are really gains and that each ounce of suffering is adding to the weight of glory, not only after this life, but also now.

15. Keep me, Heavenly Father, as the apple of your eye; defend me by your mighty power; hide me secretly in your pavilion from the fiery darts of the wicked one; and may the Holy Spirit so fill me with Christ my Lord that there may be no room for anything inconsistent with love.

16. May I not be so absorbed in my own concerns as to be indifferent to the innocent joys of children and others in my home circle.

17. Lord! I pray you'll teach me to follow where you go, to sit at your feet, and to be as true to you in times when I cannot see your face as in the glorious noon when I can see you more clearly.

18. I ask, gracious Lord, that you keep me watchful and alert, so that at any moment I may discern the movement of your hand and detect your will and guidance in the providence of little things.

19. Let me turn to you, O Lord, from the sweetest of earthly joys, to find that you are best of all, the fairest among ten thousand, and altogether lovely.

20. I draw near to you, Almighty and Everliving God, in the name of your Son Jesus Christ, my High Priest and Mediator, who is in heaven making intercession for sinners. Forgive and accept me for his sake.

21. Turn me from captivity to sin, O Lord, as the streams turn in the south. Heal my backslidings, and do not take your Holy Spirit from me.

22. O Lord Jesus Christ, give me such communion with you that my soul may continually thirst for that time when I shall behold you in your glory. In the meanwhile, may I behold your glory in the mirror of your Word and be changed into your image.

23. Help me, O Lord, daily to die to all worldly and corrupt affections and desires, that out of my death to sin there may come life to righteousness, by the grace of your quickening Spirit.

24. Teach me to be content to do your will, not looking this way or that, to compare myself with others, to seek their commendation or escape their censure. May your voice be my only law, your smile my only reward.

25. My soul wakes early and turns to you, O God, for the light. Your light is better than life; therefore, my lips shall praise you. Take my hand in yours, and make the crooked places straight and the rough places plain, that your name may be glorified in my daily walk and conversation.

26. Grant me, O Lord, the blessedness of the person whom you choose and cause to come to you.

27. O my God, my heart is overwhelmed within me. Lead me to the Rock that is higher than I. In the shadow of your wings I will take refuge until these calamities pass.

28. You are light, and in you is no darkness at all. I thank you for eyes to see, a heart to love, and a nature to enjoy your good and perfect gifts. I worship you, O Father of lights, in whom there is no variableness nor shadow of turning. Enlighten my darkness, I pray!

29. Lift me up, by your strong arm, above the mists and darkness of the valley, to stand and walk with you on the high level of your presence and glory.

30. O Father, who loves to the end, come and cleanse my feet, my hands, and lips from all corruption in my flesh and spirit. Teach me how to perfect holiness in the fear of the Lord.

31. O my Savior, I am over-tired and weary; the strain of my life has exhausted me; the pressure of daily business has robbed me of my old elasticity and spring. I have no strength even to cast my load on you. Forgive me for my lack of simple, childlike faith. Come near and give me rest. Take the burden I cannot cast on you; hush the fears I cannot allay; wipe the tears I cannot keep back.

JUNE

JUNE

1. May I not faint under your loving discipline, my Father, but accept it humbly and trustfully, so that I can become a partaker of your holiness.

2. I humbly ask that I may be so filled throughout this day with thoughts of you that this earthly life may be inspired with the spirit of Heaven. May I go about my business as one who has seen the face of God and come down to earth illuminated with the Light of Life.

3. May your companionship be so real to me, my Lord, that I may never feel lonely.

4. My one desire and prayer is that I may be filled with your love. I am bankrupt of love; I have not love enough of my own to love my neighbor as myself. Shed abroad your love in my heart through your Holy Spirit.

5. Merciful Savior, help me to pray for your children scattered in all lands, especially for those who are related to me by the bonds of nature or love. Surround them with your tender care. Keep them from harm and sin and from too great sorrow amid the disciplines of their lives.

6. I open my heart to let in your blessed fullness, O Lord; and since my capacity is small, I pray that it may be enlarged, that I may miss nothing that is possible. By love and faith, by patience and suffering, enlarge my heart, that it may be filled with all the fullness of God.

7. O Holy Spirit, help me know the joy that is unspeakable, the love that passes knowledge, and the peace that passes understanding.

8. You know my great need. Graciously draw near to me and protect me in the day of battle, that those evils which the craft and subtlety of the devil or others work against me may be brought to nothing and, by the providence of your goodness, may be dispersed.

9. Almighty God! You know that I have no power of myself to keep myself. Keep me outwardly in my body and inwardly in my soul, that I may be defended from all adversities which may happen to the body and from all evil thoughts which may assault and hurt the soul.

10. Teach me to pray, O Lord, as you taught your disciples of old; and winnow my prayers that I may desire and ask only those things which are according to your will.

11. Remember me, O Lord, now that you have come into your kingdom. Keep me true to you through this life and present me faultless before the presence of your glory with great joy.

12. You are my God, and I will praise you; you are my God, and I will exalt you. I will give thanks to you; for you are love, and your mercy endures forever. Because of your mercies, I present myself to you as a living sacrifice, holy and acceptable, which is my reasonable service.

13. May I not think too little
or too much of myself,
but soberly and rightly;
and may I give to the
world whatever you pur-
posed for me when you
created me.

14. I am not my own, but
yours, O my Master, by
your creation, your providence, and your blood.
Mark me as your servant,
that may never serve any
other master.

15. O Holy Father, make me
humble and unselfish.
Give me a childlike faith
to receive what you offer
and to bear what you
ordain; and may a new
sense of your presence
and power, through the
Holy Spirit, stay with me.

16. O true and living Vine, make me fruitful today in good works to do your will. You have given me a desire for a holy life; accomplish this by the grace of your Spirit dwelling in me and working through me continually.

17. Give to me the pilgrim spirit I must have to be in the world, but not of it. Give me grace to abstain from fleshly lusts which war against the soul. May I always obey my heavenly calling.

18. May I never forget, O Lord, that the best and happiest life must be lived in communion with the needs, sorrows, and trials of others. Give me closer sympathy with Jesus, who did not please himself, but whose blessed life was continually laid down for others.

19. Surround me behind from the pursuit of my sins and before from the assault of my foes, and lay your hand upon me to cover my head in the day of battle.

20. Deliver me, I pray, Abba Father, from the fear of others. May I fear you alone, with the fear born of love.

21. My heart is weary, O God. The strain of life, the cruel hatred of the world, and the failure of human love have left me desolate. I fall at your feet. Do not be silent, lest I go down into the pit.

22. Watch my way, Heavenly Father, and fence me around with your protecting care, that through all the changes and chances of this mortal life, I may always be defended by your most gracious and ready help, through Jesus Christ my Lord.

23. You know, Lord, how often I am sorely hindered in running the race which is set before me. May your bountiful grace and mercy come to my help, that I may finish my course with joy and receive the crown of life.

24. O blessed Lord, be the physician of my soul. Forgive its sins and heal its diseases. Lighten my heart in the knowledge of your truth; and grant me grace to pass through the remainder of this day, and through my whole life, to your glory.

25. Purify my heart, O God, by the fire of your Holy Spirit, that I may from now on please you with a pure mind and serve you with a chaste body.

26. O most Heavenly Father, send your Holy Spirit to pour into my heart that most excellent gift of love, the bond of peace and of all holiness, that I may love you with all my heart and soul and mind and strength, and my neighbor as myself.

27. Sprinkle my heart, O heavenly Priest, and cleanse my life as with pure water, that I may boldy enter within the veil and commune with God.

28. Spirit of Truth, help me to live with an unshuttered and uncurtained heart, like windows ever open to the Holy City.

29. You are stirring up my nest, my Father; the old is changing and giving place to the new. Spread your wings beneath me and teach me to trust where I can see no earthly support to rest on.

30. You know, my Savior, how I wait for footsteps that do not come; yearn for sympathy which is withheld; knock at doors that do not open; and dread what tomorrow may bring. I shrink from the loneliness of life, and the mystery of that unknown future that stretches away in the dark, like a moor beyond the light of home. But nothing can separate me from you.

JULY

1. The mountain peaks of such a life as I desire to live call to me, yet they seem too steep and high for me to reach. But you know, Lord, and you have an infinite compassion for my weakness. Fulfill in me the good pleasure of your will and the ideals you have taught me to cherish.

2. Help me, O merciful High Priest, to pray for those who have met with accident and sudden sorrow; for those who are passing through the fire, that they may not be burned; for those who are wading in deep waters, that they may not be swept down; for those who are in the midst of their enemies, that they may not be overpowered; for those who are lonely and desolate and forlorn, that they may not lose heart.

3. O you, who are the brightness of your Father's glory and the exact image of his person, may I catch some of that brightness and manifest some of that image, that people may turn from my reflection to you, the eternal reality.

4. Help me that I may not faint under your discipline or be discouraged by your rebukes, so I may at last partake of your holiness.

5. O Christ, shed light and love and life on my soul, that my being may be as pure and radiant as Alpine heights at dawn and noon and evening.

6. You, O Christ, are all I want. May your grace abound to me so that in all things at all times, I may have all I need and abound in every good work.

7. Assist me, Heavenly Father, with your grace, that my life may fulfill its possibilities and that I may walk in all the ways you have prepared for me.

8. Feed me, O Lord, with your body and blood, according to your promise, for they are meat and drink indeed. May you live in me and I in you, in ever closer union.

9. O true vine of God, I desire to abide in you, that the sap of your life, passing through my life, may bear abundant fruit for your glory.

10. Heavenly Father! Send out the tidings of your salvation to the ends of the earth. Be with your missionary servants, who are engaged in preaching the Gospel to others. Turn people's hearts to Christ, and make them obedient to the faith.

11. Heavenly Father, hurry the time when all creation will be freed from the bondage of corruption to the glorious liberty of your children, and may your purposes be quickly accomplished in your church and in the coming of our Lord Jesus Christ.

12. In your infinite mercy, O Lord, deliver me from the terror by night and the arrow that flies by day so that I may be comforted by your grace, may be guarded by your angels, and may dwell in peace and safety.

13. Gracious Father! I yield to you my will and desires, my body, the thoughts of my mind, and the aspirations of my heart. I pray that you will perfect all that concerns me.

14. May I behold your glory, O my God, until my face and life begin to reflect it.

15. O Fountain of Life, spring up in me. O Light of Life, illumine me. O Source and Sun of Love, shed your love in my heart by the Holy Spirit given to me. O Lamb of God, you who are on the throne, but who walked the rough pathway of this world, be my Shepherd.

16. O my Father, I know that you love me and that your love has chosen my path. Help me to be satisfied with your wise choice of rough and smooth, of time and tide, of sun and shower. May I finish my course with joy.

17. Teach me to do your will, for you are my God; and if I begin by choosing your will, may I end by delighting in and loving it.

18. Heavenly Father, I have been a wayward child, loving my own way and fretting too often against your will. Forgive me, I pray you; put away my sin; and make me trusting as a weaned baby.

19. Grant me, O Heavenly Father, such faith in your fatherly love and mercy that I may not be careful and troubled about the things of this life, but may seek the coming of your kingdom and the glory of our Lord.

20. In your love, my Savior, there are many benefits. Don't let my heart be troubled, neither let it be afraid. Give me the Comforter and the peace that no one can take away.

21. Bring the day of your power, O God, and speed the coming of your kingdom, that the mystery of sin may be brought to an end and all will confess Jesus Christ as Lord.

22. Have mercy, I beg you, on all who call themselves Christians. Lead them out of all their wanderings and divisions that people may see their unity in Jesus Christ and believe that you did send him to be the Redeemer of the world.

23. Dear Lord, I am poor and weak! I have nothing worth my giving or your receiving. My best is given to me by you; my holiest is ruined by sin. Take my bankrupt soul into eternal partnership with you, and say to me, "All that I have is yours."

24. Help me, O Lord, to take up my cross and follow you in the path of your humiliation and faith. So may I finally behold your face in righteousness and receive from you the crown which never fades away.

25. O Lord Jesus Christ, Captain of Salvation, who knows the hatred and workings of evil against my soul, deliver me from the manifold temptations and trials that assail me, and make a way of escape for me. Give me your mighty power, and help me to become more than a conqueror.

26. May I love you, my God and Father, with a holy, absorbing, and increasing love, not for what you give, but for who you are.

27. I thank you, O God, that your blessed Son came to destroy the works of the devil and to bring us into unity with yourself. Deliver me, I pray, from evil, and purify me even as Christ is pure.

28. Grant me grace, Heavenly Father, to abide steadfastly in your faith and fear, that at last I may be counted worthy to stand before the Son of Man.

29. Most merciful Father! I claim your covenant promise, which says that you will write your law upon my heart and remember my sin no more. May I hear you say, "Go and sin no more; your faith has saved you."

30. Pour down upon me, O God, your abundant mercy, forgiving those things of which my conscience is afraid, and giving me those good things which I am not worthy to ask, through the merits and mediation of Jesus Christ, my Lord.

31. Dear Savior, keep me from fashioning you after my own imaginings. May I not make any idol or image of you, but know you as you are.

AUGUST

1. O King of Love, let the leaves of the Tree of Life bring healing, and let your peace settle down on my harassed life like the evening calm. Minister nourishment to the weak and comfort to those who have failed. Temper the joy of success with the humility which attributes all glory and honor to your sufficient grace.

2. Lord God Almighty, how shall I ever sufficiently thank you for adopting me into your family and making me one of your children? You have taught me to know you, pray to you, and love you. You are my shield and my great reward. Bless me, and fill me evermore with the Spirit of your Son.

3. O let the great cloud of witnesses, who have gone before us and entered into their rest, be an example to me of a godly life. Even now may I be refreshed with their joy and run with patience the remainder of the race that is set before me.

4. I pray, O Heavenly Father, for those who are wandering from you in error. Have mercy upon them and bring them to yourself. Rekindle in them the flame of your pure love, and restore them to their former joy, that they may praise you for your mercy.

5. Dear Father, who knows and cares about the frailties of your people, supply me, out of your inexhaustible fullness, with all those things that I need.

6. O blessed Christ, do not let sin have dominion over me. If temptation comes, may it find no foothold in my heart; if I have to pass through scenes where the pull of sin is strong, may I not be susceptible to it; if I am strongly provoked, may I not yield.

7. Prosper, I pray, every great enterprise which seeks to promote peace, purity, sobriety, and justice between people; and think on me for good, as I do lowly and obscure things with a pure desire to please you.

8. Be, O Lord, the Alpha and the Omega of every year, month, day, hour, and act of my life. Let everything I do begin, continue, and end in you.

9. Let the fire of your love consume in me all sinful desires of the flesh and of the mind, that I may continually abide in Jesus Christ my Lord and seek the things of heaven, where he sits at your right hand.

10. In your infinite mercy, Heavenly Father, give me assurance of your protection amid the troubles of this life that I may persevere in quietness of spirit and inward peace, ever trusting in your defense.

11. Grant, O my Father, that I may remain faithful and steadfast, fulfilling the work of faith and love which you have committed to my care, that I may please you, through Jesus Christ my Lord.

12. You have given me gladness, Lord. Help me to make others glad and pass on to them the comfort with which you have comforted me. At whatever cost, may I have fellowship with you in your redemptive purpose and ministry.

13. O Lord Jesus, show me each day how I may help you in opening blind eyes, and turning people from darkness to light, from the power of Satan to God. May your kingdom come, your power work through my hands, your love throb in my heart.

14. Grant me grace, O Lord, that I may both perceive and know what things I ought to do, and may I also have grace and power faithfully to fulfill them.

15. Comforter of the comfortless, bind my soul with you in intercession! Wherever there are broken hearts, mend them; captives, release them; smoking wicks, fan their sparks; bruised reeds, make them pillars in your temple. Bless especially my loved ones, and those who misunderstand and hate me. Grant them your salvation, and meet their particular needs with your gifts.

16. Let me not be put to shame, O my Lord; but make me love and fear you with all my heart, that I may meet you with holy confidence and joy.

17. O true and only Shepherd, grant me grace, I pray, that I may never grieve your Holy Spirit or wander from the ways of your flock.

18. Fulfill in me, O God, those desires of goodness which you have put in my heart, and complete the work of faith, that Jesus Christ may be glorified in me.

19. Have mercy upon me, most merciful Father, and for the sake of Jesus Christ forgive my sins and take away all iniquity, that I may serve you from now on in newness of life, to the glory of your holy name.

20. I thank you, Heavenly Father, that I know you in Jesus Christ our Lord. He is the brightness of your glory, the express image of your person. In his face I see your face. I humbly ask that the Holy Spirit may open my eyes more fully to see, and my heart more ardently to love, you in him.

21. O Lover of all, I earnestly pray for a blessing to rest on those in prison, on those who have suffered long in hospitals without relief; on those who have the charge of young children; and on all those whose lot is thrown in distant places where the light of your Gospel never shines.

22. Make me very sensitive to perceive you, my Lord and Master, to hear your voice, and to receive the gracious inspirations which come from your heart. May the Holy Spirit glorify you, taking the things that are yours and revealing them to me.

23. O Lord, who does not despair of the most ignorant and unworthy, heal and save and teach me.

24. O Captain and Leader, may I have truth as the belt around my waist, righteousness as my breastplate, salvation as my helmet, peace for my feet, and faith for my shield. May I have no fellowship with the unfruitful works of darkness, but reprove them by my consistent life and faithful words.

25. May my heart be as a palace, which the One who is strong keeps in perfect peace. And let me not miss whatever grace may be won, or lesson learned, or sympathy gained through the fiery ordeal of temptation.

26. You are the door, O Lord! Through you may I walk to my daily work and back again to rest; and, whether in work or rest, may I abide in your safe-keeping.

27. For food and raiment; for health and mental power; for the beauty of nature; for the ladder between each lowly life and heaven; for the right to pray; for the open Bible; I bless you, O God, and magnify your name.

28. I pray for this feverish, tired world; for those who do not know you; for little children; for all who suffer and watch; for the absent, the lonely, the tired, the wayward, the sinful; for your servants who are on the point of fainting in their service. Relieve them, O Father.

29. When the storms are high, Lord Jesus, may I feel you as near as when you came through the mist and across the storm-swept waves, saying, "It is I; don't be afraid."

30. O my refuge, outside you the waves are high and the winds fierce, but in you I have haven, protection, peace, and blessedness. You are my pavilion, my refuge, my strong tower, the house of my defense, my shield and exceeding great reward. In you I make my refuge.

31. Lord, I thank you for the pillar of cloud by day and the pillar of fire by night. May I never go in front or loiter behind your presence. When it moves into the path of duty or suffering, help me to follow it; when it stays, teach me to gladly take and use the rest which you give.

SEPTEMBER

1. O my Savior, may I live in the spirit of prayer today. I sometimes get a glimpse of a life in which the heart goes out to you the whole day long, smiling to you in joy, confiding to you in sorrow, and talking with you of all the details of daily life. Graciously make such a life mine.

2. Your church, O Lord, languishes for want of times of refreshing. We are poor and needy and seek water, our tongues fail for thirst. Open rivers in the high places and fountains in the valley; make the wilderness a pool and the dry land springs of water.

3. O you who has the key of David, who opens and no one can shut, who shuts and no one can open; go before me today, I pray, opening shut gates that I may pass through them to fulfill your purposes in my life.

4. Heavenly Father, graft your Son, Jesus Christ my Lord, inwardly in my heart, that I may bring forth the fruit of holy living to the honor and praise of your name.

5. O Lord, who loves with an everlasting love, cause your light and life and love to shine into my heart, that my being may be transfigured and that people may turn from me to glorify you.

6. Grant to me, O God, I pray, the indwelling of your Spirit, that I may have a right judgment in all things, and evermore rejoice in his holy comfort.

7. You, O God, are the giver of all good and perfect gifts. To you I render all glory and praise, not only by my lips, but by giving myself up to your service and walking before you in holiness and righteousness all my days.

8. Help me to find my life according to your promise. I thank you that you have planted the germ of your own nature in me. Leave me not; neither forsake me in the toilsome, upward climb. Teach me to renew my strength and mount up with the wings of eagles.

9. Let the Holy Spirit be to me a spirit of burning, consuming the dross and selfishness and suspicion of my heart, and kindling the pure flame of warm affection towards all who name the name of Christ in sincerity.

10. O Lord Jesus, hasten the time of our homecoming, when we shall no longer be strangers and pilgrims, but will enter into the City and meet again with our beloved, through the blood of the Lamb, by which our garments are made whiter than snow.

11. Be not far from me, O Lord, this day; and through all its hours may I be found doing those things that are pleasing in your sight. May I, like Enoch, walk with God and, like him, have the testimony that I please God.

12. Almighty God, teach me the dignity of labor, the honor of industrious work, the glory of being able to do something in the world. At the best I am an unprofitable servant. Forgive, my shortcomings and failures; prosper and establish the work of my hands.

13. I bless you, O Lord, because you daily bear my burdens and load me with benefits. You are the God of my salvation; make my mountain stand strong.

14. My Savior, my heart is broken as I think of all the sorrow and pain that I have given you. But let tears of gratitude mingle with those of penitential grief as I remember your patient, abounding, unmerited love.

15. Father of Jesus, give me that same Holy Spirit, who raised him from the dead, that he may raise me also. I long that his risen life may be more evidently mine, and that I may experience the power of his resurrection, rising as a fountain in my soul.

16. My Father, may the Holy Spirit enable me to realize in daily life my true position in Christ. May I in heart and mind continually ascend and habitually dwell where he is.

17. Grant, O Lord, that through your grace the body of sin may be destroyed in me, and that through the power of your resurrection I may now walk in newness of life.

18. O God, send your Holy Spirit upon the world in mighty power to convict people of sin and righteousness and judgment. May he work again as at Pentecost, that thousands may be stricken to the heart; and may times of refreshing come from your presence.

19. O Holy Savior, make my life deeper, stronger, richer, gentler, more Christlike, more full of the spirit of heaven, more devoted to your service and glory, so that I may ever bless and praise you, and magnify your name and adorn your Gospel in all things.

20. My blessed Lord! Mercifully grant that I may follow your example of patience and that I may become a partaker of your kingdom, not only in the life which is to come, but also here and now.

21. Most Holy God, I rejoice that the Savior ever lives to intercede as our High Priest and Mediator. Through the torn veil let my prayers ascend to you, mingled with the fragrance of his perfect merit, in whom you are ever well-pleased.

22. Dear Lord Jesus! I thank you that you loved me, though most unworthy. I am the least of saints and the chief of sinners, but in the bankruptcy of my soul I trust in the exceeding riches of your grace.

23. God of my fathers, I bless you that life is a pilgrimage; that the earth is not my rest; that every day brings me nearer my home in the city of God. I humbly thank you that you are willing to be my companion in every step of the desert march.

24. Most gracious God! Help me I pray, to have a wholesome and gracious influence on those with whom I come into daily contact; diffusing in every look and gesture the sweet savor of Christ; and shedding in every act the kind light caught from his face.

25. Take my love, as the five barley loaves and two small fish, and multiply it, that it may be sweet and refreshing to you and helpful to others.

26. Holy Savior! I am often weary of myself, but I pray that you will not be weary of me. I am as the broken reed and the smoldering wick, but do not be discouraged with me; don't leave me comfortless, but come to me.

27. Enable me, O Lord, for your name's sake, to walk righteously and speak uprightly; to despise the gain of oppression and fraud; to keep my hands clean from unholy deeds; to stop my ears from uncharitable and polluting talk; to shut my eyes from beholding evil.

28. O God of peace and righteousness, may peace reign among the nations of the earth, and between human beings. May war, slavery, impurity, blasphemy, and all other evils which corrupt and injure people, pass utterly away.

29. Heavenly Father! May I use rightly the disciplines through which I am passing and learn to distinguish your meaning in every dark hour.

30. Great High Priest! I come to you with confession and faith. Do not deal with me according to my sins, neither reward me according to my wrongdoings. Teach me, through my repentance and sorrow, to hate evil more and by your grace to stand against it more carefully.

OCTOBER

1. If my soul has turned wrongly to the dark; if I have left someone wounded by the way; if I have preferred my aims to yours; if I have been impatient, and would not wait; if I have marred the pattern drawn out for my life; if I have cost tears to those I love; if my heart has complained against your will, O Lord, forgive!

2. Enable me to do not only what I like to do, but what I ought to do. May I be guided, not by emotion, but by conscience. May I be content with the limits which your providence assigns. Cause me to be faithful in little, and in common tasks to learn your deep lessons of patience, trust, and conscientiousness.

3. Father, you have loved us; you love us now; you will love us forever. Your love passes knowledge. It is like a warm, sunlit ocean enfolding the tiny islet of my life; I swim in it, but can never reach its limits. I thank you for the depth and length of your love.

4. May I delight myself in you, Almighty God. Put gladness in my heart, more than in the time when corn and wine increase. Teach me how great your goodness and beauty are.

5. Give me grace to see the beauty lying at my feet in the common places of life. Help me know that you are as near and as wonderful today as when people beheld you, Lord, when you lived on the earth.

6. Blessed Lord, may I find a balm for my own griefs and a solace for my own disappointment, in sympathy and ministry to those whose hearts are breaking around me. Give quick eye and skillful touch, that I may become like Barnabas, a person of consolation.

7. Lord Jesus, you have revealed the Father and have brought us near to God. I thank you that I may look unabashed on the glory of the eternal throne and know that all the attributes of Deity are now on my side. Good and holy are you, Lord, and I stand in you.

8. Blessed Christ! The storm is high and the night dark. Come to me, I beg you.

9. May I dwell in you, O Christ, and you in me, that you may be magnified in my mortal body, whether by life or death. In the common places of life may others see in me that which will remind them of you, my unseen Lord.

10. I beseech you O Lord, to bless those whom I love. Minister to them as I would, could I be by their side, and better than I could because your thoughts and ways are so much more tender and helpful than mine could be. Keep them safe beneath your wing.

11. Take me to your heart, Heavenly Father. Kiss me, though burdened with toil, travel, and sin. Cover me with the seamless robe of our Savior's righteousness. May I sit down at your heavenly table, and may Christ, the Door, intervene between me and the fret of the world.

12. Keep me this day without sin; into your hands I commit my life. Live in me, blessed Lord, by your good Spirit, that my life may be a messenger of helpfulness and blessedness. Supply my daily needs. Teach me to have a gracious and uplifting influence.

13. The world is dear to you, O Father. You sent your Son to save it; send your Spirit to comfort and renew. May he hover over the chaos, as he did of old upon the deep. May order and peace reign among us; and may Jesus come quickly to receive his bride.

14. My Father God, enable me to roll my ways onto you, to trust you, and to believe that when I stand with you in the perfect daylight, I will see and understand those things that now I take on trust. All your ways are mercy and truth.

15. For those I love, for all who are in sickness and sorrow, for those who anticipate this day with anxiety; for those who are called to suffer, to undergo special trials, to pass through the valley of the shadow, I humbly pray that they may be provided as they need.

16. Great, wonderful, and gracious Father, I am tired of working, striving, thinking; and so I fall back on your love, more tender than a mother's and as lasting as your own eternity. I cannot save this world or carry its weight. Hold me in your loving arms.

17. O Divine Lord! When I am most absorbed in my necessary business, may you not withdraw your presence, but be permanent and abiding. May I be faithful to you in little things, following the inner light until it leads me into the perfect day.

18. Heavenly Father, I ask you to give me faith in your guardian care. May I realize that I am surrounded by hosts of watching angels. Bless and defend and save all those I love, that they may be conscious partakers of your heavenly blessing.

19. I desire, O Lord, to take on your yoke and to learn your secrets. Teach me to rejoice always, to pray without ceasing, and in everything to give thanks.

20. I give thanks to you with my whole heart and sing praises to your name for your lovingkindness and your truth. Bless the Lord, O my soul, and all that is within me bless his holy name! Hallelujah, for the Lord God Omnipotent reigns!

21. I pray for my companions in life's pilgrimage: for the feeble and the dying; for the despondent and the oppressed; for the poor and sick and forlorn. May their valleys of weeping become filled with springs of joy.

22. O Light of Life, shine upon my heart, that pines for the summer of your love. May all your blessed saints, who gather around you in the world where night never comes, find in you their true consummation and bliss. Be to me what you are to them; and let me find in you the foretaste of heaven.

23. Undertake for the oppressed and weak, for women and children, for slave and the prisoner. Watch by the bedside of the sleepless. Solace the heart of the bereaved. Hasten the coming of your kingdom, and the gathering of your elect.

24. O Lord, who illumined the heart of Thomas with the clear radiance of your risen glory, you know how to deal with the doubts and perplexities of my heart. I have not seen you as Thomas did; give me the blessedness of those who have not seen and yet believed.

25. May I become a pillar in your temple, inscribed with my own new name. May I be clothed in white garments and be like gold refined by fire. Make me pure in your holiness and more than a conqueror through your blood.

26. O you, who sat at Jacob's well, give me to drink of the water of life, and to hear your voice which is as music; and let that spring, of which you speak, rise within my heart to eternal life.

27. On this new day I adore you, my God and Father. The light is your garment; the heavens are the curtains of your home; the clouds are your chariot; the winds are your messengers; the fire is your minister. From you and through you and to you are all things. To God be the glory.

28. Holy, holy, holy, are you, O God! Heaven and earth are full of your glory. Every day is a day that you have made. May I hunger no more, neither thirst any more, because I am satisfied with the abundance of your house, and have drunk from the river of your pleasure.

29. You are a covenant-keeping God! Your faithfulness reaches to the skies; help me to count on it in every step of this day's pilgrimage. Your righteousness is like the great mountains; may I keep it in view always.

30. My Master and Lord! May I know that you go before me as you went before your disciples. The sword pierces your heart before it touches mine, and the waves spend themselves on you before I am wetted by their spray. The heavy part of my cross rests on you.

31. Make me to hate evil and to cling to that which is good. Take away my heart of stone, and give me a heart of flesh. Deliver me from my idols. Take away my love of sin. Put your Spirit within me, and cause me to walk in your way.

NOVEMBER

1. Gracious Lord, forgive the past. Keep me as the apple of your eye. Surround me with your guardian care, and let your highest purposes be realized in me. So will I offer in your tabernacle sacrifices of joy. I will sing, yes, I will sing praises to the Lord.

2. I adore you, Holy Father! There is no limit to your power or to your love. You are greatly to be loved! There is none like you, glorious in holiness, fearful in praise, doing wonders. Accept the homage of my soul and life, through Jesus Christ.

3. O God! Make me increasingly conscious, I ask you, of the indwelling of your Holy Spirit. May he witness with my spirit that in spite of all my sin I am still your child; may he enable me to die to the solicitations of the tempter.

4. Accept what I have done for your church and glory, great Lord. Though it be little in the eyes of humanity, may it be much to you. Teach me to remember that I am a priest and to realize that every sphere may be a temple to service and each act a sacrament.

5. May your Word be increasingly precious to me, O Lord; and in your words may I ever hear the Word. Beholding your face in this mirror, may I become changed.

6. There are so many mysteries in the world and in life, O Lord. My eyes are tired of straining into the dark. I can only follow on to know you, but I believe that your going forth is as sure as the morning. In the meanwhile, refresh my heart as the rain.

7. Yours, O Lord, is the greatness and the power, and the glory, and the victory, and the majesty; for all that is in the heavens and the earth is yours. Yours is the kingdom, O Lord, and you are exalted above all. Glory to you!

8. Gracious, Holy Savior! Cleanse my tears, purify my penitence, refine my hope, and accept me as needy and helpless, who can claim nothing. I count on you because you have bidden all who are weary and heavy-laden to come to you.

9. Holy Savior! Undertake the care of our failures that might lead us to despair, and the joy of our successes that might induce pride. Make right what is wrong; undo what is done amiss; establish, strengthen and prosper all you can use.

10. Lord Jesus! Teach me how to apply to the common things of daily life the heavenly principles of the risen life. May I think of nothing as common or unclean. May every common bush be aflame with God.

11. Keep me, O Lord, this day, free from known sin. May I fall into no sin, neither run into any kind of danger; but may all I do be ordered by your governance so that I may do that which is pleasing in your sight.

12. Heavenly Father! Deal not with me according to my sins, negligences, and ignorances. Cleanse my defiled soul and unclean garments. Do not forsake the work of your own hands. Perfect that which concerns me because your mercy endures forever.

13. Heavenly Father, put all my sins behind you into the depths of the sea. Deliver me from the love of sin. Cause all grace to abound to me, that I may in all things and at all times have all I need and abound in every good work.

14. Eternal God! As my outward body decays, may the inward person be renewed day by day; and may my light troubles, which are but for a moment, work out for me a far more exceeding and eternal weight of glory.

15. Lord Jesus, I pray for your one church, the members of which are scattered in many different denominations and over the wide world. We who are one with you must be one with each other; but grant that our unity may stand revealed and confessed, so that all people may believe.

16. The good I want to do, I do not do; the evil that I do not want to do, I do. I grieve for my temper, my pride, my self-will, the bad thoughts I permit, the unkind, things I say. But you knew all this before you awakened me. Have compassion and save me!

17. Take me as I return home to you, soiled and dusty with the sin and business of the day. Cleanse me from all unrighteousness, not only with the grace of forgiveness, but also with the grace that passes through every chamber of the inner life, purifying and sanctifying all.

18. Heavenly Father! I thank you for the gift of your Son, who is the Pearl of Great Price; the Hidden Treasure, which makes the soul rich forever; the Delight of Heaven; the Glory of his church; the All-sufficient Portion of his own.

19. Heavenly Father, bring the reign of your Son in every land; may all rulers fall down before him, all nations serve him. Let his name endure forever and be continued as long as the sun, and all humankind be blessed in him.

20. Teach me, O Lord, the way of your commands, and I shall keep them to the end. Give me understanding that I may keep your law. Help me stay on the path of your commandments, for in them I delight.

21. If it is your will that temptation should come to me today, may I not distrust your leading hand, nor think that failure is inevitable, nor concern myself too much with our great adversary. Be with me when I am surrounded by the wild beasts of temptation, and let angels minister.

22. Hear my prayer for our leaders and our country, for those who exercise authority, or enact laws, or pronounce judicial decisions. Enlighten those who teach the young, or write books, or edit newspapers. Give peace in our time, good Lord, I ask you.

23. Forgiving Savior! If I have in my heart something against my brother, may I have the grace of silence concerning it to others and the grace of speech about it to him alone. Let the love that covers a multitude of sins be mine.

24. Holy Father, I mourn the divisions which divide your people, and humbly ask you to fulfill the prayer of our blessed Lord, that those whom he purchased for his possession may all be one, even as you, Father, are in him and he is in you.

25. Blessed is the one whose strength is in you, my God, and in whose heart are your ways. May that strength be mine, yet not mine, but yours perfected in my weakness. May my heart be strong to hope, to love, and to endure.

26. O strong Son of God, who is like the sun coming out of his chamber, and rejoicing as a strong man to run his race, draw me into fellowship with you in your strength and love, and in your tenderness toward the weary and weak.

27. To you, Heavenly Father, I commend my comrades and friends on every part of life's great battlefield. Let no defeat discourage them. Let no sudden temptation overcome them. Let no long-continued sorrow wear out their loyalty or discourage their faith.

28. O blessed Master, make me like you, in your ceaseless intercessions, for your church and for the world. Let it not be enough for you to pray for me, but pray in me. Let your prayers for others also pass through my lips.

29. O God, who hears prayer, let the voice of supplications be always audible in my spirit. May I pray with faith, so you can entrust me with the key of your treasury.

30. Though my outward life be a desert march, may my heart live in the heavenly places, which Jesus, the forerunner, has entered. May I eat of the fruit of the land, and drink of the river of God, and have unbroken victory over all opposition.

DECEMBER

1. My Savior and example, I pray for those who misunderstand and injure me; for any I have wronged; for those to whom in past days I may have been a stumbling block; for those who might have been saved if I had been more faithful. Do for them by other means what I might have done.

2. Forbid, O Heavenly Father, that I should ever lose the freshness, fertility, and beauty which you can maintain in hearts which are open to you. May it be my lot today, in the pressing duties of daily toil, to have a fresh, holy, and fragrant spirit.

3. For all your gracious care I reverently thank you; and if you have permitted things to happen which have tested me and filled me with bitterness, help me to trust in your infinite love, that through the discipline I may give up all that grieves you.

4. O Savior, forgive my sins, my faithless tears, and my repining complaints; my thoughtlessness of others and my self-centered anxiety. Lift me on to the tide of your love and up to fuller, richer, deeper levels of experience.

5. Great Shepherd! Lead me to the pastures of tender grass and by the waters of rest; or if my way lies among rocks and desert places, support me with blessings of goodness. Let your rod and staff be my comfort.

6. Quickly come, Lord Jesus, to right the wrongs of time and establish your everlasting kingdom. Grant to me, though unworthy, to sit with you at your heavenly table, and see you when you are crowned in the joy of your bride, the church.

7. How great is your goodness, O God, which you have stored up for those who fear you, which you have worked for those who trust in you! For from you and through you and to you are all things, and to you shall be the glory forever.

8. Lord Jesus! Make the fountain of my heart pure, that the streams may be pure also. May my heart compose good things, that my mouth may speak of our King. May my conversation be seasoned with grace, full of truth and love and strength.

9. You make your dwelling, O God, with those who have a humble and contrite spirit and who tremble at your word. Take my weakness up into your strength, my ignorance into your wisdom, my changefulness into your everlasting constancy.

10. Gracious Father, I thank you for the Son of your love, for all that he has done for us, and will do; for all that he has been to us, and will be. I thank you that he holds me in his strong, pierced hand, loving me with the love that cannot let me go.

11. My Father, teach me to trust your love. May I dare to believe in it when the dark clouds build as well as when the sun shines. May I never doubt that you are doing your best for me and that what I do not know now, I shall know hereafter.

12. Great Creator! I am nothing better than common earthenware; but may I be cleansed and purified and filled with your heavenly treasure. Dip me deep into the river of life, and give refreshment through me to many parched and weary hearts.

13. Great Lord of all! I pray for this great world, especially for those who in distant lands are sharing your gospel. Bless them in their work and encourage them when their hearts are faint. May they remember that they are fellow-workers with you.

14. Holy Spirit, may my heart be filled with your love, my lips with gently helpful words, and my hands with kind, unselfish deeds. May those who see me know that I have been with Jesus. May the fragrance of his presence be spread in every act.

15. I humbly ask, O Christ, that your peace may be the garrison of my heart with its affections, and of my mind with its many thoughts, that it may ever rule over the tumultuous passions that build in me. And out of this peace may I rise to serve.

16. Giver of peace! May peace be in this house; peace be in the homes of those who love me; peace be with the tired workers and lonely pilgrims and sin-weary hearts; your peace, Heavenly Father!

17. You have taught me to look for the time when all creation shall be made free with the glorious liberty of the children of God. Bring that glorious day, O Lord, when your own hand shall wipe tears from all faces and the former things will pass away.

18. Gracious Lord! May the Holy Spirit keep me ever walking in the light of your countenance. May he fill my heart with the sense of your nearness and loving fellowship. Order my steps in your way, and then walk with me. Teach me to do the thing that pleases you.

19. Father, my heart is somewhat apprehensive when I contrast the spirit of your blessed Son with the storm and strife of life; but be with me, and may my soul keep its Sabbaths.

20. Great Burden-bearer, I bring to you my anxieties and cares about myself and my dear ones; about my body and soul; about the things of this life and those of eternity. I cannot carry them; they rob me of peace and strength. Will you take them, Heavenly Lord, and carry them for me?

21. Great Savior, who sent the Comforter! For the temptations which he has overcome in us; for the comfort he has given us; for the fruits he was worked in us; for the glimpses of your love he has unfolded; and for the hopes he has inspired, I lovingly thank you.

22. Great God! Teach me the art of so living in fellowship with you that every act may be a psalm, every meal a sacrament, every room a sanctuary, and every thought a prayer. May the bells that ring to common duty be inscribed with "Holiness to the Lord."

23. Most blessed Lord, may all uncleanness and filthiness, foolish talking, covetousness, bitterness, malice, and anger be put away from me. May I forgive, even as God in Christ has forgiven me.

24. Bring the coming of your kingdom, and to this end help every true worker for you, the world over. May the kingdoms of this world speedily become the kingdoms of our God, and of his Christ. Help me to speed the coming of that day.

25. O you who sent your Son, may the purity, simplicity, and beauty of the Holy Child, Jesus, be poured out like a sweet fragrance through our hearts and lives. Bless those absent and those we love, the strangers and the lonely; and may we all meet in the great homecoming.

26. O Savior, I commend to you those whom I have injured, or spoken against, or failed to help. I pray for those who have treated me wrongfully and despitefully. I intercede for my dear ones, for all sufferers and mourners, and for your saints everywhere.

27. Blessed Lord, may I be strong, not for myself alone, but for others. Teach me to bear the frailties of the weak, to surround those that are overwhelmed in the fight of life, and to lighten the load of care beneath which many of my fellow believers are pressed.

28. Holy Spirit, make me merciful in my judgment of others. May I think no evil. Deliver me from the spirit of retaliation. Help me to speak and think of others as I would have them speak and think of myself. Make me pure in heart; not only in my outward walk, but also in my inward temper.

29. Keep me, O gracious Master, from the corruption and lust of the world. May my speech be always full of grace, seasoned with salt. May my behavior always become the gospel of Christ. May there be nothing in my loneliest moments to put you to shame.

30. O Head of the church, I would intercede on behalf of all who are ministers of your holy gospel. Enrich them with knowledge and articulation. As they break the living Bread, may they be nourished. As the river flows through them to others, may it keep their hearts fresh and fruitful.

31. You have brought me, gracious God, through the year. Accept my deep and loving thanks. I trust you for what you have withheld as I bless you for what you have given. May goodness and mercy bring me to the many mansions you have prepared, and may you be near me until the end.